WHAT TO DO WHEN WHEN EVERYTHING FALLS APART

Van Crouch

What to Do When Everything Falls Apart
ISBN: 978-1-936314-51-5
Copyright 2011 by Van Crouch Communications
P.O. Box 320
Wheaton Illinois 60189
www.VanCrouch.com

Published by Word and Spirit Publishing
PO Box 701403
Tulsa, Oklahoma 74170
wordandspiritpublishing.com

Contents

Introduction

Does fear have you paralyzed? Are you afraid to take risks and explore new ventures? Have you become convinced that success comes easily to others...but it eludes you? Has adversity driven you to the point of giving up?

There are times in our lives when we wake up and realize we're not the success we planned to be. Problems seem to pile upon problems, worries upon worries, and fear begins to set in. It may be harder to sleep, and you may even feel like crying. You may wonder, *does anybody really care?*

I know these feelings because I've been there too. At some point in our lives, we all come to a time when we are genuinely tested by a period of despair. It may be the breakup of a marriage, a loss of a job, a serious illness, or the even the death of a loved one. These times can cause us to become better...or bitter.

So why do some people grow despondent and quit, while others refuse to let tough times defeat them? Why is it that some people manage to turn their problems into possibilities? Some seem to grow during tough times, to learn from them and overcome overwhelming odds, and then step back on the path of success, happiness, and hope.

And more importantly, how can you be this kind of person—the kind who gets up when you've been knocked down?

What to do? This book provides a simple set of guidelines—eight concepts to break the gridlock of panic and paralyzation. When you feel like everything around you is falling apart, these are the eight things God helped me with and that I think He desires to share with you, too. Here is the insight and inspiration you need to build new dreams from the disappointment of your life.

No matter what is going on in your life, it isn't final. Your troubles have a limited lifespan. It's time to get up and dust yourself off, because *here's what to do when everything falls apart!*

WHAT TO DO WHEN EVERYTHING FALLS APART

1

Turn to Jesus

There was a time in my life when everything was falling apart. My career was faltering and my marriage was failing. I was depressed, despondent, and discouraged...and those were my strong points!

You may have been there too—you may even be there right now, which means you picked up the right book. What do you do when things aren't working out? You could read any old self-help book...but will that really help? You know, I went to a major bookstore one day and asked the clerk to point me in the direction of the self-help books. "No," he said, "that would defeat the purpose!"

If you have that feeling that everything is falling apart and you don't know where to turn for help, I have some good news. This is a book of ideas that may seem simple but are proactive steps that can help you if you feel like a piano player in a marching band.

Maybe you feel like you are raising the kind of children you don't want your kids playing with. Maybe you're struggling in a relationship, or you have received a negative report from the doctor. Maybe you're struggling financially, or with emotional problems—all at the same time!

If you have that feeling that everything is falling apart and you don't know where to turn for help, I have some good news. This is a book of ideas that may seem simple but are proactive steps to get you back in the game and in a position to win.

So What Do We Do?

I love the Bible because despite being thousands of years old, it still speaks to our everyday life. I want you to take a look with me at the story of someone who had come to a point in his life when everything was falling apart. In Matthew 17:14-21, we meet a man with a serious problem.

Jesus and His disciples were in the middle of a crowd when a man walked up to Him and dropped to his knees. He said, "Lord, have mercy on my son, for he is an epileptic and suffers severely; for he often falls into the fire and often into the water."

Can you imagine this as a parent? Not only does his son have seizures, but they put his life in jeopardy.

The man goes on to say, "So I brought him to your disciples, but they could not cure him."

I can almost hear the exasperation in Jesus' voice as He replied, "O you unbelieving (warped, wayward, rebellious) and thoroughly perverse generation! How long am I to remain with you? How long am I to bear with you? Bring him here to Me" (Matthew 17:17 AMP).

What an invitation this is! You may have a problem that from your perspective seems unsolvable, just as this man must have felt about his son's situation. But the same invitation that Jesus extended to this man is the one He wants to extend to you as well.

The very first and most important step is to make a quality decision to come to Jesus.

Jesus did not come against the father or the son with the problem, He went after the spirit that was causing the problem. The Bible tells us that "Jesus

The very first and most important step is to make a quality decision to come to Jesus.

3

rebuked the demon, and it came out of him, and the boy was cured instantly."

Obviously some of the problems that we experience in life can be cured instantly—thank God for instantaneous healing! This happens when the Word of God and the power of God come up inside of you and are bigger than the problem.

The Word of God and His life inside you are like immunity or a vaccine. We don't read stories in the news about people dying from polio these days. We read about the importance of the vaccine, of having it inside of us. Like any immunity or vaccine, it rises up within us when we are confronted with disease, driving it away and preventing it from sickening our lives.

Now, you might think that by healing his son, Jesus had solved all of this man's problems. But I think the problem went deeper, and it included the very disciples themselves at this point in Jesus' ministry. You see, the disciples privately asked Jesus, "Why could not we cast it out?"

The leading healing evangelists and people with a deliverance ministry of his day had failed publicly to heal his son. Now listen to Jesus' answer—why could they not drive it out? "Because of your unbelief." *Unbelief.* In the Amplified version it says, "Because of the littleness of your faith [that is, your lack of firmly relying trust]. For truly I say to you, if you have faith [that is living] like a grain of mustard seed, you can say to this mountain, 'Move from here to yonder place,' and it will move; and nothing will be impossible to you."

The father's problem here probably seemed unsolvable. If he was like many parents, his son was one of the most important things in the world to him, and his seizures threatened his life daily. And the disciples could not help him because of the smallness of their faith and because they had not done the preparation to be ready for this level of crisis—extensive prayer and fasting.

After the disciples failed to heal his son, this man must have thought, *What am I to do?* His problem must've seemed insurmountable, his best hope exhausted. Like this man, you may be thinking, *Where do I turn?* Which direction do you go, to whom do you turn?

The devil is a thief, he comes to steal, kill, and destroy, and he will try to keep you stuck in your valley and from gaining any momentum in life. Right now you may feel like you're down in a dark valley in your life. But if you are down in the valley, I want to encourage you to look up on the mountain. Someone is walking down into your dark valley, and He brings with Him the light. And the darkness cannot stand before the light!

The psalmist David said, "I will lift up my eyes to the hills—from whence comes my help? My help comes from the LORD, who made heaven and earth" (Psalm 121:1). David raised his vision and his perspective above his problem and put his eyes on the Lord.

You may feel very alone right now, your life in broken pieces around you, but the same Jesus who healed this boy and to whom David looked for his help is the same Jesus the Bible promises will never leave you or forsake you (Hebrews 13:5). In Matthew 28:20, Jesus says He will be with you until the end of the world. Hebrews 13:8 says that Jesus is the same yesterday, today, and forever, so none of these promises have lost their power or perfection.

He watches over His Word and hastens to perform it.

In Jeremiah 1:12 God gives us the great promise that He watches over His Word and hastens to perform it—for those of you who don't speak King James, "hasten" means that He won't waste any time. If the promise is in His Word, God will see it happen in your life.

So where do you turn when everything is falling apart? Jesus. He is the way, the truth, and the life, and He is the path to the Father (John 14:6).

Poor Alternatives

Our world offers endless possibilities, but I guarantee that this father in Matthew had explored all of his world's potential fixes and ways of healing his son. But none of them had been able to set him free. His world—this little boy—was as vulnerable as his next seizure, which might cast him into the fire or the water and snuff out his young life.

So what do you do if your whole life is falling apart and the things that are precious to you are on a knife's edge, threatening to fall into the fire on one side or the water on the other?

You do the very same thing this father did—you go to Jesus.

I told you that there are eight things that are guidelines for getting through the periods of life where everything seems to come crashing down around us. Turning to Jesus is by far the most important of all, but in the next few chapters I'm going to give you seven more obtainable, doable steps that you can follow when life has you on the ropes. I have put them in the form of questions that you should ask yourself, but for this to work you must answer these questions with brutal honesty and spend the proper amount of time thinking them through, because in them I believe you will discover the keys that will unlock the power and blessings of God in your life.

2

What's in Your Heart?

It starts with me. When everything seems to be falling apart, the first place you look is within your own heart. When things are not developing the way you'd hoped, the first person to look at is yourself. If your vision is not coming to pass for your life and it isn't developing like you expected, you need to take a look at your own life. I've noticed that when I point my finger at someone else as being the source of my problems, I've got three pointing right back at me.

We've got to keep it real. We must honestly assess our own hearts. If we have allowed envy, jealousy, strife, or anger to come into our lives, we have sown the seeds of our problems within our own lives.

In Psalm 139:23-24, the psalmist says, "Search me [thoroughly], O God, and know my heart! Try me and know my thoughts! And see if there is any wicked or hurtful way in me, and lead me in the way everlasting" (AMP).

David, the man after God's own heart who wrote that psalm and so many others, was not the poster child for life without problems. When confronted by Nathan the prophet after he committed adultery with Bathsheba and had her husband, Uriah, murdered, David didn't blame Bathsheba for taking a bath on her roof. He didn't talk about "our" mistake or about what "we" did.

David showed his heart by immediately repenting and saying, "Have mercy on me, oh God" (Psalm 51:10). David could have tried to hide behind extenuating circumstances, but instead this man who loved God cried out for mercy and later wrote, "Search me, O God, and see if there is any wicked way in me." This should be the template for us when things are going wrong and we rightfully recognize that we have played a role in our own crisis.

Give no place to the devil.

Ephesians 4:27 says, "Give no place to the devil." Blaming others and not owning your stuff gives place to the devil, but the devil should only have one place in our lives—under our feet! We must make sure that we do not open the door to the devil.

10

Don't Go over the Hedge

You may be familiar with the story of Job in the Bible. Everything fell apart in his life as the devil came against him. How did the devil get in? In Job 1:10 we read the devil accusing God of having put a hedge around Job and everything he had.

In Job 3:25, he said, "For the thing I greatly feared has come upon me, and what I dreaded has happened to me." What had happened? The devil had bet that Job would curse God if God allowed the devil a place in Job's life. God knew that he wouldn't, and Job acknowledged his own responsibility and later said that he had said things he knew nothing about and that were far too wonderful for him. Job's pride in questioning God contributed to this fall.

Fortunately, there's a happy ending, because when Job finally learned how to close his mouth, he received back from God more than double everything he had lost.

When we give place to sin in our lives, we let the devil up from his place under our feet and give him permission to run amok in our lives. Any time we violate any of God's Top Ten or commit any other sin, we can bring consequences into our lives.

Ephesians 4:26 says, "Be angry, and do not sin: do not let the sun go down on your wrath." My wife and I have figured this one out—we made the decision not to let the sun go down on our wrath...so we stay up and fight till dawn! The other night was our date night, and my wife said, "Why don't you take me somewhere I haven't been in a while?" I said, "How about the kitchen?" We're trying to be more romantic, so we bought a waterbed. My wife has nicknamed it the Dead Sea!

First Corinthians 11:28 is a well-known Communion passage and says, "Let a man examine himself." This is in reference to taking the Lord's supper, and Paul is reminding us to be sure that we make things right with God so that we don't take it in an unworthy manner, opening ourselves to judgment, sickness, and worse.

But examining yourself and asking God to search your heart is only one element—what do you do with what you find in there?

When I was a new Christian I regularly went to the altar to repent for my sins, but on one occasion the Lord called me on it. I felt like God asked, "What are you doing?"

I thought, *I'm repenting.*

This is not a joke: I felt like God said, "You're down here having a good cry and using up more than your share of the Kleenex, but you're not repenting. You're practicing remorse."

I asked the Lord, "What's the difference between repentance and remorse?"

God called me on the carpet. He impressed on me that I was down there at the altar having a therapeutic event and feeling sorry for the things I liked to do. But there was no intent in my heart to actually change. When I was done, I got back up and went back to my seat the same way I was when I came.

Repentance is not feeling sorry for what you have done; repentance literally means changing your mind. You change your mind so that you can change your direction and ask God to work a heart-change within you. When we do, we come up to live on top with Him; when we just feel sorry for ourselves, we just wallow in our guilt and condemnation and nothing changes in our hearts.

Jesus said it is what comes out of our hearts that defiles us—evil thoughts, murder, adultery, all sexual immorality, theft, lying, and slander

(Matthew 15:18-20). All this and so much more comes from our hearts, and if we don't ask God to search our hearts and root all this junk out, we will not experience the kingdom of God like He desires for us.

When things are falling apart in your life, you have no further to look than what you say. Jesus tells us that you can know a tree by its fruit and that out of the "abundance of the heart the mouth speaks" (Matthew 12:33,34). "A good man out of the good treasure of his heart brings forth good things," Jesus goes on to say in the next verse, "and an evil man out of the evil treasure brings forth evil things."

Death and life are in the power of the tongue.

Proverbs 18:21 says, "Death and life *are* in the power of the tongue, and those who love it will eat its fruit." So listen to the words that are coming out of your mouth. If you hear bad fruit, it's because there are things in your heart that God needs to uproot and replace. "Replace with what?" you might ask. So glad you did!

Paul tells us that "the Holy Spirit produces this kind of fruit in our lives: love, joy, peace, patience, kindness, goodness, faithfulness, gentleness, and self-control" (Galatians 5:22-23 NLT).

If your life is falling apart, you'd be wise to look for the telltale signs of the fruit of the spirit in your life. Ephesians 4:32 says we are to "be kind to one another, tenderhearted, forgiving one another, even as God in Christ forgave you."

If this isn't what is coming out of your mouth, take a hard look at your heart to see if you've inadvertently opened the door to this bad fruit. If you've let the enemy come in and kill, steal, and destroy...it's time to put a stop to it.

I hope you're burning with curiosity about how to do that, because I can't wait to tell you—but I'm going to make you wait for the next chapter!

3

What Has God Promised?

When everything around you is coming crashing down, the very first thing you must do is go to Jesus. And as we discussed in the previous chapter, next is asking Him to search your heart and learning to watch your own heart and mouth to see what's coming out of it.

So what's next? You need to check up on the promises of God—you've got to know what He said in His Word.

The Bible says that each of us should "be diligent to present yourself approved to God, a worker who does not need to be ashamed, rightly dividing the word of truth" (2 Timothy 2:15). But one day it occurred to me that if we can "rightly divide" the Word of God, then the implication is that we can wrongly divide the Word as well.

Some people seem to want to get God's Word to say what they want it to say. Instead, we must let the Word of God say what God intended for it to say—and then put it up like a mirror in front of our faces and use it to impact our lives, change our hearts, and turn our situations around.

Paul cautions us to not just listen to God's Word. We must do what it says. Otherwise, we are only fooling ourselves. For if we listen to the Word and don't obey, it is like glancing at our face in a mirror. We see ourselves, walk away, and forget what we look like. But if you look carefully into the perfect law that sets you free, and if you do what it says and don't forget what you heard, then God will bless you for doing it.[1]

Always remember, your faith comes by hearing the Word of God (Romans 10:17). And it's going to take serious faith to walk through your broken world, because if you're like me, your problems didn't show up overnight. Since most of them didn't show up suddenly, most of them don't go away suddenly either.

In every case, I've had to let the Word of God build my faith and change my thinking so that I begin to talk like God talks—because only then can I walk like He walked, have what He said I could

---

[1] See James 1:22-25.

have, do what He said I can do, and be the child of God that He's called me to become!

See, we can fully trust Him to do His part. Numbers 23:19 says, "God is not a man, that He should lie, nor a son of man, that He should repent. Has He said, and will He not do? Or has He spoken, and will He not make it good?"

Ticked Off? Grieved in the Spirit? The Results Are the Same

One of the areas I've had to deal with in my own life regarding God's promises is that too often I've believed God for too little. You'd think that after walking with Him all this time, I'd know better, but all too often I find I'm just like the children of Israel.

We read the Old Testament account of these guys, and we think, "Boy were they dumb!" They experienced nearly every miracle you can think of—the plagues of Egypt, the Red Sea opening before them, bread appearing from thin air every morning, rocks that gave water, and game birds landing in their camp. God led them by the hand, at night as a pillar of fire and by day as a cloud. And boy did they need direction; it look them forty years to make an eleven-mile walk. What does that show me? That

They should have been saying, "God can!"

men have been refusing to ask for directions for a very long time!

But even after experiencing all of God's miraculous provision, still they griped and doubted, saying, "Can God prepare a table in the wilderness?" They had the audacity to say, "Can God?" when they should have been saying, "God can!"

And all too often, we do the same. We read this account of the Israelites and can criticize them for their unbelief, but if we're not careful, we can do exactly the same thing. The Bible says they limited the Holy One of Israel[2]—and it ticked Him off—and we must be careful that we do not do this ourselves.

We've got to go back to the promises of God and say not only God can, but God *will*! We must diligently search the Word to show ourselves approved, find where it is written, and then believe God! We've got to nail some promises down for our situations and the challenges we face...and then stand on the Word of God without doubting or wavering.

---

[2] See Psalm 78:41.

Don't tick God off by thinking small or being ignorant of His promises! Those promises are the ammunition you need against the enemy and your circumstances, so you must study them. Learn them! Get them inside your heart so that when everything is falling apart you have them to turn to. Don't turn to a shoulder to cry on first, or your therapist first, or your escapism first; turn to the Holy One of Israel, who is faithful to fulfill even the smallest portion of His Word!

You've got to get the Word inside of you however you can! But getting inside isn't enough; you've got to do it. And it must—must, must, must—affect how you speak. It isn't enough just to hear it. It must change your life and your speech.

Let's take a look in the next chapter at the next point I want you to consider when everything is falling apart. We touched on it earlier, but this is so important we're going to revisit it. When you're in trouble, what you find coming out of your mouth is a good indicator of whether or not you're really getting the Word inside of you and becoming a doer of it.

4

What Are You Saying?

In the first chapter I told you that we must examine our hearts and ask God to do the same, just as David prayed. And then I briefly touched on the fact that you can often tell what's in your heart—by listening to what's coming out of your mouth. Jesus tells us that out of the treasures of the heart, the mouth speaks.

The Bible goes so far as to say that we're snared by the words of our mouth and that the power of life and death is in the tongue.[3] What we say is important and it is crucial that we keep our confession in line with the Word of God.

When some Christians hear the word "confession," they get turned off. They've heard it called "name it, claim it," "blab it and grab it," or "say it and see it." Maybe they've even seen it abused, but whatever you call it, the fact is that these principles and precepts work. And honestly, when your whole

---

[3] See Proverbs 6:2 & Proverbs 18:21.

world is collapsing, you cannot afford to ignore the power of what you say.

Even the secular world has clued into the power of what we say—in the business and motivational world, they call it "positive self-talk" or "positive affirmation." They've discovered the principle, and they don't even understand the power behind it! We Christians should know how this works, because it's in the Bible, yet all too often we forget there is a miracle in our mouths waiting to happen.

James makes this statement in his famous description of the power of the tongue, which you really need to go read. He says, "Indeed, we all make many mistakes. For if we could control our tongues, we would be perfect and could also control ourselves in every other way" (James 3:2 NLT).

The word "perfect" here means "mature," and believe me, it takes a mature Christian to watch his tongue and begin using it for blessing and not cursing. You'll remember from earlier that Jesus said that a good "tree" bears good fruit—so what kind of fruit is coming from your lips? If it's praises for God sometimes—say when everything is going right—and curses at other times, it's time to go back to chapter two and ask God to search your heart!

Let's Move Some Mountains

So let's say you've asked God to search your heart, and you're beginning to watch your tongue. It's easy to say, "Don't say negative things," and only catch the tip of the iceberg of what God would like to accomplish through your tongue.

Jesus was so bold He made a crazy-sounding promise: if someone speaks to the mountains in his life and says, "'Be removed and be cast into the sea,' and does not doubt in his heart, but believes that those things he says will be done, he will have what-

It's time to start confessing what God says is true.

ever he says" (Mark 11:23). It's not enough to just stop saying your doubts; it's time to start confessing what God says is true as bigger than the seemingly insurmountable mountains in your life!

Most people say what they have...when they could have what they say. Now, I know that confession has been abused in some circles over the years, and I know that some people have taken it to extremes or made it superstitious in a way that God never intended. But to ignore the power Jesus promises us we have is to ignore one of the single greatest powers God has provided us for life-change on this earth!

Jesus promised that we have "whatever" we say, so I am committed to lining up my speech with the Word of God. You must understand, you are the prophet of your own life, and what you say over a situation may well be the determining factor in your end results. Can you afford to not take this promise completely seriously?

Use Your Words to Bless Others

One of the abuses I hear people complain about when they hear confession out of context is that they often hear selfishness—that people who buy into this are only using it to acquire things for themselves or trying to control their lives in a way that's at odds with the rest of the Word. While some do this, God has indeed provided this as a way for us to bring His will into our lives.

But that's just our lives, and the same way I can say that if you're simply cutting out negative talk you're only scratching the surface, if you're only using this principle for your own benefit, you are missing a large portion of what God has intended for His people.

I use my words to encourage people whenever I can. Not long ago, I was visiting a Texas prison, speaking to men on death row. I wanted to encourage them, so I gave a talk on how to set short-term goals. One man told me that he was headed to the electric chair. I told him, "Well, more power to you!" No matter who you are or what situation you're in, you have people to whom you can speak and encourage.

You've got to speak the best and believe the best. People who need your encouragement are everywhere—friends, family members, a waitress, the cop giving you that ticket. You can have a ministry of encouragement no matter your own life situation.

You might say that you have tried to encourage people before—but they didn't receive it. You're missing the point! *You* get encouraged! What they receive is between them and God; what you give, likewise, is between you and God. If you use your words to encourage others, you're not looking for feedback from them, you're looking for feedback from *God*.

You must learn to speak your desired result. Think about your words—are you saying what God says about your situation? Or are

You must learn to speak your desired result.

27

you saying what you see with your physical eyes? You've got to keep your eyes on Jesus!

You remember Peter, trying to walk on the water to Jesus? He was doing just fine…as long as he kept his eyes on Jesus. He was going down! But he had the presence to shout out to Jesus, "Save me!"

That might be where you are. You're going down with all hands on deck. It's time to stop confessing your circumstances and to start crying out to the One who can save you! Get your eyes off the wind and the waves, and fasten them firmly on Jesus Christ and what He has to say. He seemed to think that Peter could walk on water, and Peter did too…as long as he was eye-to-eye with Jesus.

Get your eyes off of what's going wrong. Anyone can state the obvious. But it takes a mature Christian to watch your tongue and make the decision to confess what God promised in His Word is true. Do this—cry out to Him—and immediately He'll reach out to you and right that sinking feeling.

Think of your words. Are you saying what God says in your situation? And while you're considering that, think on this: if you're in a fight, where are you fighting? If you're fighting from the firm footing of

God's Word, you've got backup. If you're fighting on your own terms—you could be in for a pretty big fall.

I think it's time to learn how to pick the ground for your battles.

5

What Arena Are You Fighting In?

You can't always pick your battles. Sometimes your child doesn't want to eat his dinner, and no matter how tired you are, it's going to be a fight to get him to do what is right. Your load at work might not be yours to choose, your daily commute might not be something you can do much about, and you may not have much say about the doctor's report on your health. You may find yourself in a situation where you're deeply in debt.

However, when you're engaged in a struggle you can always choose how to fight. If you fight in the arena of faith, then no weapon formed against you will prosper (Isaiah 54:17). But if you fight in the arena of reason, you'll almost always be defeated.

Go for the home court advantage. Operate by utilizing the power of a strong, Bible-based church with a pastor who's excited about the things of God.

A long time ago I fought a battle to get out of debt. I had bills that I didn't have money to pay and

31

no idea how I would cover them. Was I broke? No, I was working my way up to broke!

Those were tough times, and the bills piled up on the kitchen table. As I focused on the bills and fretted about how I would ever get any of them paid, I became more and more discouraged. Then one day I read a book in the Old Testament even many Christians I know had not heard of: Malachi. In there I found a very interesting conversation where God said something that caught my attention.

Basically, God said, "I'm getting ripped off." "Who, you?" they asked. God replied, "Yes, Me." But His people didn't understand. "How?"

And here's what got me: "In tithes and offerings."

But God did not leave them hanging without explanation...or promise. He told them exactly how to do it: "'Bring all the tithes into the storehouse, that there may be food in My house, and try Me now in this,' says the LORD of hosts, 'if I will not open for you the windows of heaven and pour out for you such blessing that there will not be room enough to receive it'" (Malachi 3:10).

But don't stop reading there. He goes on to say, "And I will rebuke the devourer for your sakes" (Malachi 3:11).

I learned that God was the one who gave me the power to get wealth and be successful in that if I would listen to His commands and obey Him I wouldn't have to chase His blessings—they would overtake me![4]

When you face a struggle and it feels like everything in your life is falling apart, you must quit trying to battle in the natural and instead pick the ground on which you fight: the supernatural. You must fight in the arena of faith, where "God shall supply all your need according to His riches in glory by Christ Jesus" (Philippians 4:19).

You must fight in the arena of faith.

"Now faith is the substance of things hoped for, the evidence of things not seen," we read in Hebrews 11:1. You've got to have some hope! Because when we fight in the arena of faith we are not relying on

---

[4] See Deuteronomy 8:18 and 28:2.

our own weapons; we place our trust in God's supernatural weapons.[5]

If you want to win, you must pick the ground on which you fight your battles and you must have hope, because hope will change your life.

When you fight with faith in God, if you are down, you can get up.

When you have hope, if you are lost, you can be found.

If you have faith and you're sick, you can be made well.

If you have hope when you're broke, God can restore your finances.

God can give you the vision when you have no direction, a purpose when you are adrift, and a reason to hope when everything seems hopeless. How can you have hope when everything is falling apart?

Simple: faith. It's the substance of things hoped for, the evidence of things not seen.

---

[5] See 2 Corinthians 10:4.

God-pleasing Faith

I don't know about you, but "just" having faith isn't enough for me; I want to have faith that pleases God. Want to please God? I'll show you how: "But without faith it is impossible to please Him, for he who comes to God must believe that He is, and that He is a rewarder of those who diligently seek Him" (Hebrews 11:6).

This is pretty basic. Who does He reward? Those who diligently seek Him. What happens to those who diligently seek Him? He rewards them.

Get out of the arena of the natural and all the limits of your circumstances, put on the armor of God, and get into the arena of faith in an incomparable God. Simply His names tell us so much about who He is:

>Jehovah Tsidkenu, our righteousness!
>Jehovah Makaddesh, our sanctifier!
>Jehovah Shammah, our presence!
>Jehovah Shalom, our peace!
>Jehovah Jireh, our provider!
>Jehovah Rapha, our healer!
>Jehovah Nissi, our banner!

Jehovah Rohi, our shepherd!

El Shaddai, our all-sufficient source!

Those names should get you excited! They're the promise that whatever you're facing, God is there to meet your need.

A final note on faith: faith isn't denial. Having faith doesn't mean problems don't exist. Problems do exist! Jesus said that in this world you will have trouble. But the best part is He didn't leave it there! He goes on to say, "Take heart, because I have overcome the world" (John 16:33 NLT).

When you fight in the arena of faith, you understand that even through problems do exist and we will go through them, the God we serve is bigger than all our problems! Got big problems? Get your eyes off the problems and onto God, because when you focus on the problems, they get very big. Instead, get your eyes on God and watch your problems shrink before the power of the Lord of Heaven's Armies, our All-Sufficient One!

The God we serve is bigger than all our problems!

Now, for the next point, I want to cover something even more practical. We've looked at turning to Jesus, asking Him to search our hearts, learning His promises, and watching what you say. Now that I've told you about the importance of fighting in the arena of faith, it's time for one that might hit close to home. When everything is falling apart, you have to look at those who are around you—not to point fingers or blame, but because the quality of those around you is very important. They can lift you up...or they can pull you down. So which is happening in your life?

6

Who Are Your Companions?

In the previous chapter we talked about the importance of knowing which arena you're fighting in and ensuring that you're fighting in the arena of faith, because you will only win if you're placing your trust in God completely. That is what it takes to please Him—having faith and knowing He rewards those who seek Him.

As important and even practical as living in faith is, now I want to cover a topic that seems a lot more like something your mother would say: you've got to be careful about whom you let close to you.

I was once on a crowded elevator when a fellow in the back said, "Phew! Someone's deodorant isn't working!" A bright bulb said, "It's not me. I'm not wearing any." I say that because it's funny, but also because it hides a major truth: who you are around influences the nature of your environment.

Your companions can have a major influence on your life. Take Jesus for example: He had seventy disciples at one point; fifty-eight quit, leaving Him with twelve, and one of those betrayed Him. But within those twelve, He had a Peter, a James, and a John, three pillars of the early Church.

If you're like me, once you started going to church and had the Word of God planted in your heart, you learned that certain family members and friends were fine with you getting saved...they just didn't want you getting too saved. And then when you began to develop vision and destiny, about the time you got really excited about an opportunity to step out deeper in your walk with God, Uncle Ralph showed up.

Uncle Ralph is on relief. He considered his fifth-grade year his senior year, and he uses his fishing license as his valid form of identification. His side of the family tree doesn't fork, and the light actually comes on when he leaves the room.

But that's never stopped him from stating his opinions. Uncle Ralph's going to tell you what he thinks you can and can't do, what you should or shouldn't do, and what he heard the man with all the answers on the radio say about what God can't do, wouldn't do, couldn't do, or shouldn't do.

Uncle Ralph has mental B.O.—stinkin' thinkin.' But he's family, and so many of us are vulnerable to him and others in our lives who throw a wet blanket on our burning excitement for God. The role of Uncle Ralph in your life might be your boss or co-workers, the other moms you get together with while the kids play, or an old buddy or girlfriend from school.

You cannot help but be influenced by the people you're around. You become like the people you hang with.

The Bible tells us that "bad company corrupts good character" (1 Corinthians 15:33 NLT). And if you need any confirmation about the importance God places on this, just read the first Psalm:

Blessed is the man who walks not in the counsel of the ungodly, nor stands in the path of sinners, nor sits in the seat of the scornful; but his delight is in the law of the LORD, and in His law he meditates day and night. He shall be like a tree planted by the rivers of water that brings forth its fruit in its season, whose leaf also shall not wither; and whatever he does shall prosper. (Psalm 1:1-3)

The people you spend time with rub off on you. But let me tell you this, as well: it can be easier to stay away from the wicked, habitual sinners and tactless mockers than it is to avoid soured Christians.

Especially when you're newly saved, you think everyone is as on fire for God as you are. You don't know that there are some real downers out there, hiding in the pews and seats around you in the Body of Christ. There are quite a few professed Christians who have mental B.O. just as badly as Uncle Ralph, and if you spend too much time rubbing up against their defeated, unbelieving, and tapped out attitudes, it will begin to impact your life.

If everything is falling apart around you, the last thing you need is one of these people who have turned away from pleasing God with their faith and instead have fully bought into the world's way of doing things. All they see are the wind and the waves; they've lost sight of Jesus, and they're sinking fast.

And if you don't watch with whom you spend time, they'll pull you down during the very time you most desperately need people around you who will bear you up!

In Mark 4:24 Jesus says, "Take heed what you hear."

Faith comes by hearing, and hearing by the Word of God.

So what should you be hearing? As we read earlier, "Faith comes by hearing, and hearing by the Word of God" (Romans 10:17). What you should be hearing is the same as what you should be speaking—the promises of God. These come from that old leather book—the B-I-B-L-E, and only here will you find the words of life.

Jesus makes it pretty clear: "It is the Spirit who gives life; the flesh profits nothing. The words that I speak to you are spirit, and they are life. But there are some of you who do not believe" (John 6:62-64).

Some people don't believe! They may go to church, they may say the right things, they may even look the part, but down deep they don't seem to have any life. While Uncle Ralph may discourage you by giving his uneducated opinion, professed Christians with no life can be some of the most dangerous companions you can keep, because they're in disguise. They should build you up, but instead they end up tearing you down.

You shouldn't be surprised when people in the world don't understand your hunger for the things of God. When they have a problem, they don't turn to God—but at least they're honest about it. Christians with no life, who do not believe, profess one thing but do another. These are the ones to look out for.

So what do you do? How can you tell who to trust? You've got to seek out the people who pray with you in faith. You'll usually find them at churches that preach the Word, where there is life and things of God are going on. They'll get excited when people come to Christ, will freely offer to pray with you, bear your burdens, and will encourage you to turn to God, search your heart, learn His promises, speak those promises over your situation, and fight in the arena of faith.

When everything is falling apart around you, find some of these people to pray with you in faith. You must have friends that will hook up with you and believe God with you and for you so that together you get into the realm of the Spirit instead of the flesh. You need friends who refuse to back down in the face of rough circumstances and who will cling to God's promises and encourage you to do the same.

Now, all of this is not to say that we aren't called to go out into the world and make disciples of Jesus Christ. However, if you're beat up and bruised by a life of troubles or heartache, you need to be built up. In the same way you can use your words to lift your life up but must also use your words to encourage others, living the words of life Jesus teaches in front of others, boldly despite your circumstances, can have a great effect on the people around you.

Anyone can be cheerful when things are going well; anyone can praise God when everything is personal pan pizzas or five-dollar footlongs and everything is going their way. But when life's troubles come, the difference between us and the world is that we turn to God and we overcome by the blood of the Lamb and the word of our testimony!

Thank God for your friends who have not had the benefit of the training in the Word that you have, or who haven't been in a good church like I pray you're in. Love them! Be kind! Just know when you are beaten down or in a foxhole with life's troubles bombarding your life and the enemy coming your way, you need warriors next to you who are empowered by the Holy Spirit. When everything is falling apart in your life, you want companions who will stand with you and believe with you, surrounding you with faith and love.

So now that I've gotten off my pulpit regarding the company you keep, I want to touch again on something I covered briefly earlier. It isn't enough to just listen to God's Word. You mean there's more to it? Yes! Let's talk about that for a little bit in the next chapter.

7

Are You Doing the Word?

I hope you're getting something out of this, because these points that God shared with me were vital for bringing me through times where my life seem to have collapsed around me.

Earlier in the book I talked about the importance of looking into the "mirror" of the Word in order to begin reflecting in your life. But I want to come back to an important topic, because it isn't enough to just hear the Word. You must do what it says! You can surround yourself with great people and do many of the things I've talked about so far, but if His Word is just what you say and not what you do, you're missing the point.

Not only that, while the Bible is "profitable for doctrine, for reproof, for correction, for instruction in righteousness," the Word is to prepare and equip us for doing every good work.

God says, "I will watch over my Word, and hasten to perform it" (Jeremiah 1:12 KJV). So God will do His part—He will do whatever He said He would do, and He will do it in His perfect timing.

Are you obeying the scriptures that will produce victory?

God has His end covered, and if you're putting the Word in so you can say the promises of God out, you've started participating in a way that will bring you victory. But right now some of you are thinking, *Does this mean I have to memorize the whole Bible? What if my life is ending right now and I don't have that kind of time?* The beauty is we serve a big God—far bigger than all our problems. He has graciously given us a way that we can participate with Him in fixing them. So what you must ask yourself is, "Are you obeying the scriptures that will produce victory in your life?"

If you don't have time to memorize the whole thing, you must make time to focus on claiming the promises to not just get through...but to more than overcome!

Start with some like Philippians 4:6-7, which says, "Be anxious for nothing, but in everything by prayer and supplication, with thanksgiving, let your requests be made known to God; and the peace of

God, which surpasses all understanding, will guard your hearts and minds through Christ Jesus."

Another translation puts this so well, saying, "Don't worry about anything; instead, pray about everything. Tell God what you need, and thank him for all he has done. Then you will experience God's peace, which exceeds anything we can understand. His peace will guard your hearts and minds as you live in Christ Jesus."[6]

This is such an amazing promise! What, don't worry? Pray about it instead? Believe God that He will actually bring peace to your troubled heart? If you bought into this and fought in the arena of faith, God will watch over this promise and hasten to perform it!

Or how about this one from Ephesians 6:10: "Finally, my brethren, be strong in the Lord and in the power of His might," Paul tells us. How? "Put on the whole armor of God, that you may be able to stand against the wiles of the devil." What is this armor, and what does it do? So glad you mentioned it!

---

[6] New Living Translation

Put on every piece of God's armor so you will be able to resist the enemy in the time of evil. Then after the battle you will still be standing firm. Stand your ground, putting on the belt of truth and the body armor of God's righteousness. For shoes, put on the peace that comes from the Good News so that you will be fully prepared. In addition to all of these, hold up the shield of faith to stop the fiery arrows of the devil. Put on salvation as your helmet, and take the sword of the Spirit, which is the word of God. Pray in the Spirit at all times and on every occasion. Stay alert and be persistent in your prayers for all believers everywhere. (Ephesians 6:13-18 NLT)

We put on God's armor because we aren't fighting flesh and blood enemies; we're fighting the devil and his evil minions. To stand firm, we must use the spiritual weapons God has given us to resist spiritual foes.

James tells us of what I call the "Law of the Draw." He explains that God resists the proud but gives grace to the humble and then tells us, "Therefore submit to God. Resist the devil and he will flee from you. Draw near to God and He will draw near to you" (James 4:7-8).

Want to resist the devil with the armor of God that Paul talks about? Then borrow a page from James' playbook and humble yourself and draw near to God. Submit to God, resist the devil. Over the years, I've learned that the more I submit, the less there is to resist. God must increase in our lives, and we must decrease.

There are so many great resources for gathering the promises to address your specific situation. Many pastors have preached on topics from healing to financial increase, and in addition to their recordings there are great books on the subject.

However, nothing is a substitute for searching the Bible for yourself for God's promises to you. When God makes a promise from His Word apply to you specifically, we call it a *rhema* word, and this is very powerful. Search your Bible's concordance for topics that apply to your situation, or use technology to search for promises on the Internet.

As you get the Word inside of you, don't forget how important it is to then do it and not just read about it. God is always faithful; He will keep his end of the deal. Your job is to believe Him, arm yourself with equipment He has provided, and stay in faith. He will watch over His Word and is always faithful to perform it!

In this next and final chapter I want to address something that is both an attitude and an action: praising God. When things are good, it's easy. But if things were good, you probably wouldn't have picked up this book, so I think there are some final things that God showed me you may need to read.

8

How Is Your Praise Life?

The final thing that God showed me is that just as it's important to ask God to search our hearts and to do all these other things, it's vital that we are honest with ourselves about our praise. Are you praising God?

Some people say, "I will thank God when things get better." But if you want things to get better, you'd better start thanking God now! Paul tells us, "Rejoice always, pray without ceasing, in everything give thanks; for this is the will of God in Christ Jesus for you" (1 Thessalonians 5:16-18).

> *Rejoice always, pray without ceasing, in everything give thanks.*

Remember Paul and Silas in the Roman jail? They had been beaten with leather straps embedded with chips of bone or metal so that every lash cut their backs open. It was the middle of the night, and Paul was hurting—you and I probably cannot understand how much pain he was in. His legs were most likely locked in irons, and the disgusting, dirty cell was pitch black. He couldn't see his hand in front of his face, but he could hear the rats and probably felt them nibbling at his feet.

And this wasn't even Paul's worst day! Then right in the middle of this mess, Paul said, "Silas, are you there, brother?"

Silas replied out of the darkness, "I'm here, Paul." He hurt as badly as Paul did.

"Silas," Paul began, "I feel something."

"It's just the rats," Silas answered.

"No," Paul said. "I feel an halleluiah coming on."

"Now? In jail?" Silas asked.

"Right now," Paul answered. And then he started—voice hoarse, body filled with pain. Silas joined in, and the whole prison heard these two crazy men praising God in the middle of the night and their stinking, rat-filled cell.

And do you know what happened? The whole jail started shaking! God loves to hear the praises of His people, and no circumstance on earth can stop Him from moving heaven and earth when we open our mouths and fill them with the Word and praises to Him!

The whole prison shook, the shackles came off, and the doors swung open—the impossible happened, and the insurmountable obstacles proved no match for God. Not only did Paul and Silas go free, the guard and his whole family were saved, too!

No matter our circumstances, we must always praise God. Anybody can sing a tune on a clear day at noon, but our lives aren't always rosy. There are times it's cold and damp, we hurt and don't feel like cracking our mouths (unless it's to groan). But those are the times when we must praise God as an act of our will.

We don't just worship God when we feel like it. If you wait until you feel like it, when everything is falling apart...you might be waiting for a very long time. But the sooner you praise God, the sooner you'll start experiencing the breakthrough that will make you want to sing at the top of your lungs!

So What's Your Excuse?

Sometimes what we've experienced in the past provides an excuse for not praising God. You may feel disqualified from God using you or doing anything in your life because of what you've gone through. We can sometimes get the impression that God only uses those with perfect pasts, but nothing could be further from the truth.

Moses was a murderer and couldn't even speak well—he had a stuttering problem. David, a man after God's own heart, slept with another man's wife...and then had him murdered to try to cover it up. Paul hunted Christians until his experience on the Damascus Road. Timothy was too young, and Abraham and Sarah were too old. John was self-righteous, and Peter was a waffler. Jacob was a liar, and Jeremiah was suicidal. Jonah ran away from God, Hosea married a prostitute, and Elijah was a burnout.

So what's your excuse? Some people blame their home lives—"My family was messed up," they say. Join the club! Hardly anyone starts on good footing, and for those who do, something else goes wrong.

Here's the deal: God never consults your past to determine your future.

We can always let something stifle our praise. The enemy will always help you with an excuse, but you must remember the importance of being a doer of the Word and not just a reader. When someone who is committed to obeying the Word hears, "Rejoice always, pray without ceasing, in everything give thanks; for this is the will of God in Christ Jesus for you" from 1 Thessalonians 5:16-18, there's no room for excuses. It's His will, so you do it.

You may be going through the worst season of your life. You might not know which way to turn—just like the man and his epileptic son who helped us begin this book. Paul and Silas were beaten within an inch of their lives, but they knew the difference between you having a problem...and a problem having you. They also knew to turn to Jesus. The man with the epileptic son in Matthew came to Him in person, and Paul and Silas came to Him in praise.

Worship Releases Miracles

We began the book with a story about a desperate man seeking Jesus' help for his son. Now I'd like to show you the story of a woman who turned to Him both with praise and in person and what Jesus did in her life as a result because she wouldn't take "no" for an answer.

57

In Matthew 15:21-28 we read the story of a woman with a daughter possessed by a demon. You don't hear as much about deliverance ministry as you once did, but years ago I was ministering to a lady in a service. I knew she was afflicted with a demon, so I said, "You foul spirit of gluttony, I command you to come out in Jesus' name!" All was quiet, and then a small voice said, "I'll come out…for a cookie."

The very next person in line had a spirit of procrastination. That one took longer to come out— it kept saying, "I'll be out in a few minutes."

Delivering people from demons was a very real part of Jesus' ministry on earth, but He came to minister to God's people, the Jews, first. The woman we're about to read about was not a Jew.

In Matthew 15:21-28 we read, "Then Jesus left Galilee and went north to the region of Tyre and Sidon. A Gentile woman who lived there came to him, pleading, 'Have mercy on me, O Lord, Son of David! For my daughter is possessed by a demon that torments her severely'" (Matthew 15:21-22 NLT).

When the man whose son had a demon causing his epilepsy came to Jesus' disciples and then to Jesus, He ministered to him right away. But listen

ESCRITURAS DE SANIDAD

Bendice, alma mía, a Jehová…y no olvides ninguno de sus beneficios. Él es quien perdona todas tus iniquidades, el que sana todas tus dolencias. Salmo 103:2-3

Éxodo 15:26	S. Marcos 16:17-18
Éxodo 23:25	S. Juan 9:31
Deuteronomio 7:15	S. Juan 10:10
Deuteronomio 30:19	Romanos 8:11
Josué 21:45	II Corintios 1:20
Salmo 91:16	II Corintios 10:4-5
Salmo 103:1-5	Gálatas 3:13-14
Salmo 107:20	Efesios 6:10-17
Salmo 118:17	Filipenses 2:13
Proverbios 4:20-23	II Timoteo 1:7
Isaías 43:25-26	Hebreos 10:23
Isaías 53:5	Hebreos 10:35
Jeremías 30:17	Hebreos 13:8
Joel 3:10	Santiago 5:14-15
Nahum 1:9	I Pedro 2:24
Malaquías 3:10	I Juan 3:21-22
S. Mateo 8:2-3	I Juan 5:14-15
S. Mateo 18:18-19	III Juan 2
S. Marcos 11:23-24	Apocalipsis 12:11

VAN CROUCH

COMMUNICATIONS

P.O. Box 320 • Wheaton, IL 60189-0320
Phone: 630-682-8300 • Fax: 630-682-8305
Email: vancrouch@aol.com • www.vancrouch.com

HEALING SCRIPTURES

Praise the LORD, O my soul, and forget not all his benefits
— who forgives all your sins and heals all your diseases.
Psalm 103:2-3

Exodus 15:26	Mark 16:17-18
Exodus 23:25	John 9:31
Deuteronomy 7:15	John 10:10
Deuteronomy 30:19	Romans 8:11
Joshua 21:45	II Corinthians 1:20
Psalm 91:16	II Corinthians 10:4-5
Psalm 103:1-5	Galatians 3:13-14
Psalm 107:20	Ephesians 6:10-17
Psalm 118:17	Philippians 2:13
Proverbs 4:20-23	II Timothy 1:7
Isaiah 43:25-26	Hebrews 10:23
Isaiah 53:5	Hebrews 10:35
Jeremiah 30:17	Hebrews 13:8
Joel 3:10	James 5:14-15
Nahum 1:9	I Peter 2:24
Malachi 3:10	I John 3:21-22
Matthew 8:2-3	I John 5:14-15
Matthew 18:18-19	III John 2
Mark 11:23-24	Revelation 12:11

VAN CROUCH

COMMUNICATIONS

P.O. Box 320 • Wheaton, IL 60189-0320
Phone: 630-682-8300 • Fax: 630-682-8305
Email: vancrouch@aol.com • www.vancrouch.com

to what happens here: "But He answered her not a word. And His disciples came and urged Him, saying, 'Send her away, for she cries out after us.'" When this woman came to Jesus, He didn't even respond to her! And the disciples, who had never gone to a sensitivity training seminar, just got annoyed at her begging. I'm sure Jesus was very gentle when He finally did answer her: "I was not sent except to the lost sheep of the house of Israel."

But this lady didn't quit. In fact, in the face of this hardship, she did something rather remarkable: she worshiped Him. In Matthew 15:25 we read her response: "Then she came and worshiped Him, saying, 'Lord, help me!'" In her difficulty, in her desperation, she worships the Son of God, even though it doesn't look like she's going to get the answer to her request.

Jesus answered, "It is not good to take the children's bread and throw it to the little dogs." Ouch! But read her response very carefully: "Yes, Lord, yet even the little dogs eat the crumbs which fall from their master's table."

Worship released her miracle.

And then Jesus gives the most amazing answer: "O' woman, great is your faith! Let it be to you as you desire.' And her daughter was healed from that very hour'" (Matthew 15:28). Worship released her miracle.

Worship Even When You Don't Feel Like It

Paul and Silas began to sing when they had no reason to do so whatsoever. Nothing about what had happened to them would make you feel like singing. Yet in the darkness with the rats for company, that's exactly what they did—they started singing.

Praise began filling up that cell, drifting through the bars and floating out over the city of Philippi. As they continued to praise, their worship soared into the atmosphere and rose right into the very throne room of God.

In heaven, God said, "I hear a song."

"Of course you do," Michael said, "this is heaven. Everybody is singing up here!"

God said, "No, this is different. This is the sound of my children singing when they've got no reason to sing. That's the sound of men praising Me when they have no reason to praise!"

And as He listened to their worship, the angels got excited and God began tapping His foot. The

Bible says that heaven is God's throne, but the earth is His footstool. So when God began tapping His foot, He started rocking the planet and the doors and shackles came wide open! And not only did Paul and Silas go free, God set the jailor and his whole family free as well!

When we praise, miraculous things happen for us...and those around us! You may not know which way to go or where to turn. But if you'll begin to worship the Most High God no matter your circumstances, He will begin to rock your world! He will lift you above the fog and smog of this world when you put your confidence in the Word of God. God will always come through! God will set you free, throwing the gates of your prison open and shattering the bonds that hold you!

When everything falls apart, praise the Lord. Don't run...except to God. Don't look anywhere else except the Word. And then knock and keep on knocking and ask and keep on asking. If Jesus was moved by a Gentile woman's faith—the faith of someone to whom He was not even called—how much more will God surely hear the cries of you, His blood-bought child?

And not only will He deliver you—when you praise Him no matter what your circumstances are like, He will use you to set others free as well!

9

It's Time for Your Breakthrough

I want to leave you with some final thoughts of hope, and to convince you that no matter how bad things have been, new beginnings are possible. Some people may scoff at this, but that just means they don't understand the exceedingly great power God has to outperform their wildest expectations.

If there is any doubt within you that God can breathe new life into your situation, I'd like to share with you a couple of scriptures that have meant a lot to me. One is in Ezekiel 37, which I strongly encourage you to read in your own Bible.

The Lord took the prophet Ezekiel and led him to a valley covered in dry human bones. The Lord asked him if those bones could live again and he wisely replied that only God knows the answer to that. What's interesting here is how God goes about performing a mighty miracle. He does so... through the words of His chosen man.

God says, "Speak a prophetic message to these bones and say, 'Dry bones, listen to the word of the Lord! This is what the Sovereign Lord says: Look! I am going to put breath into you and make you live again! I will put flesh and muscles on you and cover you with skin. I will put breath into you, and you will come to life. Then you will know that I am the Lord'" (Ezekiel 37:4-6 NLT).

As Ezekiel repeated this promise just as God told him, God's Word proved true. Ezekiel obeyed the Word of the Lord, and God worked at the impossible. Dry bones lived again. The passage wraps up by saying, "'I will put My Spirit in you, and you shall live...Then you shall know that I, the LORD, have spoken it and performed it,' says the LORD" (Ezekiel 37:14).

> *I will restore to you the years that the swarming locust has eaten.*

In another place, the Lord promises, "So I will restore to you the years that the swarming locust has eaten" (Joel 2:25). The Lord has spoken! The dry bones of your life can live again, and He will restore to you what has been lost, just as He did with Job.

These are amazing promises from an all-powerful God. There is nothing impossible for Him, including the restoration of your life. But you must be willing to do what He says. Proverbs 29:18 says, "When people do not accept divine guidance, they run wild. But whoever obeys the law is joyful" (NLT).

God provides this guidance through His Word and Holy Spirit. He sent Jesus to pay the price for us so that we could be restored to Him and more than overcomers. It is in overcoming that you are prepared for promotion, but God's grace for you can be in vain if you do not respond to Him. You're no longer a victim, so you must quit acting like one!

Jesus guaranteed your overwhelming victory on the cross, but now you must walk it out. Just because you have made mistakes does not mean that you are a mistake! He died for your mistakes—they're already paid for.

But you must have hope for your future. If you don't, you'll be powerless in your present. You must trust Him enough to line your life up with the Word of God. His Word contains all the promises you need, but you must look for them and then speak them over your life. When you embrace His promises, I guarantee that you'll be too anointed to be disappointed!

Conclusion

I have spent this book trying to show you why some people refuse to let tough times defeat them and in fact turn problems into possibilities. Those who overcome all the adversity this world can throw at them are people who turn to Jesus first.

They have learned to look in their hearts and ask God to search them and know them and point out any wicked way in their lives. They have learned what God has promised in his Word...and then put it on their lips. They've learned to fight in the arena of faith. They choose godly companions who build them up and encourage them in that faith. They have learned to obey the Word and do it. And they have learned to keep praises on their lips even when times are hard.

Jesus told us that hard times would come—we will have trouble in this life. There is no magic bullet that will prevent it; there are only those who deal with the trouble God's way...and those who do not.

I don't ascribe to know everything, but I do know this: God is a good God, and the devil is a bad devil. They've never traded places and never will.

In Ephesians 3:20-21, Paul tells us, "Now to Him who is able to do exceedingly abundantly above all that we ask or think, according to the power that works in us, to Him be glory in the church by Christ Jesus to all generations, forever and ever Amen."

How much is God able to do? Infinitely more than we might ask or think! This means that we must be asking and thinking...and we must do so at a higher level than we have been. Whatever you can dream, God can outperform—which says to me that if I dream big, God is dreaming even bigger!

I pray that by this point in the book you are finding new reasons for hope and that these pointers that God gave me will provide guidelines for turning your situations around. Remember an important key: Paul and Silas did not wait until they were out of prison before they began worshiping God.

Also, the Hebrew children who would not bow to King Nebuchadnezzar's statue and whom we recognize in Hebrews 11 as being heroes of the faith understood a powerful concept. They told the king they would not bow because they knew God would save them. They had hope and faith. But they also had a strength of character that they demonstrated when they said that even if God did not save them, they would still do the right thing and would never bow and worship a false god.

Many things can be a false god in our world today. We can try to use psychology to replace Him, or think that sound financial planning will prevent us from ever having a rainy day we can't handle. Some people turn to watered-down versions of touchy-feely spirituality that really isn't true to our Lord Jesus at all.

Do not bow to your circumstances!

Do not bow to your circumstances! Don't bow to the world's way of doing things. Commit to doing it God's way and watch Him outperform your wildest dreams!

Remember that the first and most important thing is turning to Jesus. If you cannot remember anything else, remember that—every other thing I said in this book can really come back to that one oh-so-important statement. Put Him first, and everything else will follow. Put Him first, and He will put back together the broken pieces of your life. Your dry bones can live again!

A Prayer of Agreement

If you did not feel like everything has fallen apart around you, you would not have picked up this book. And I don't want to leave you with just guidelines and no support. In fact, I would be honored to agree with you in prayer wherever you are and at whatever point you are reading this book. Read the prayer below and ask Jesus to be with you as you pray it, because it says in the Word that wherever two or more are gathered together in His name, He is there.

Father, right now in Jesus' name, I thank You for my friend who has picked up this book because of great need. We always need You, but especially right now when everything seems to be falling apart.

Lord, we turn to you first. Search our hearts and reveal to us if there is any wicked way. Teach us Your Word and promises, and put a guard over our mouths that we would speak only blessings and never curses. Help us to stay in the arena of faith where You have so mightily equipped us with Your armor and made us more than conquerors. Help us to obey the scriptures that we know and show us in

Your Word the *rhema* word that will change our lives. Help us to worship You no matter how we feel and to praise You in any and every situation.

Father, help us to be like the woman who wouldn't take no for an answer and to knock and keep on knocking, knowing that You withhold no good thing from us and that You promise that if we seek You, we will find You.

Right now, we place ourselves in agreement with You and Your Word. Right now we believe You for breakthrough in every impossible situation exceedingly abundantly above everything we could ask or think. We thank You that this breakthrough is beginning right now and that You will watch over Your Word to perform it and that You are faithful to complete the good work You have begun!

We choose to praise You and to thank You for Your total and complete victory on the cross. You are exalted, the devil is defeated and under my feet, and Jesus Christ is Lord to the glory of God the Father!

I pray all of this in the authority and power of Jesus' name. Amen.

About the Author

 Van Crouch is widely regarded as one of the best and more versatile speakers in America. As the founder and president of Van Crouch Communications, Van challenges individuals to achieve excellence in their lives. After ranking as a consistent sales leader with the American Express Company, Van went on to receive many awards for outstanding performance in the insurance industry and has been a qualifying member of the Million Dollar Round Table.

Van is the author of several bestselling books including *Stay in the Game, Dare to Succeed, Take It Back, Winning 101, The C.E.O's Little Instruction Book* and *Storehouse Principle.* Van is in demand for his thought-provoking seminars and keynote engagements to Fortune 500 companies, government organizations, professional and collegiate sports teams, churches and para-church organizations, and management and sales conventions worldwide.

Van Crouch has the ability to motivate people to raise their level of expectation. He will cause your attitude to become more positive, your problems smaller, your self-esteem and confidence will grow, and your self doubts disintegrate. He is sure to both inspire and challenge you. Van and his wife, Doni, reside in Wheaton, Illinois.

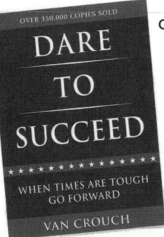

Churches • Conferences • Banquets
Staff Training • Men's Meetings
Christian Business Seminars
Ministers' Conferences

VAN CROUCH
COMMUNICATIONS

P.O. Box 320 • Wheaton, Illinois 60189
Phone (630) 682-8300   Fax (630) 682-8305
Email vancrouch@aol.com

www.vancrouch.com

With over **350,000 sold**, *Dare to Succeed* is now newly revised and updated to inspire a new generation of readers. Worldwide motivational speaker and author, Van Crouch conducts engagements for national athletic organizations like the Chicago Bears, Fortune 500 businesses, and nationally known ministries including Focus on the Family. Filled with Van's uniquely humorous style, inspiring stories, and powerful quotes, *Dare to Succeed* gives readers the motivation they need to go to the next level.

> *Van Crouch is one of America's great speakers and authors. His amazing humor combined with practical insight will have you not only encouraged, but empowered. Crouch is a must read for all those desiring to change their future today!*
> —Gregory M. Dickow
> Life Changers International, Chicago, Illinois

> *I truly appreciate your interest, leadership, and time spent in furthering and interpreting the "Good News." Please continue to help and inspire our people in the coming year. Thank you again for a job well done.*
> —Mike Ditka
> ESPN Sports

> *Van, you have not only challenged and inspired us, but you have enabled us to more insightfully seek the path in both our personal and professionallives.*
> —Dr. James Dobson, PH.D.
> Founder, Focus on the Family

FEATURES AND BENEFITS:

* *Dare to Succeed*, with more than **350,000 copies sold**, is now newly updated and revised to motivate and inspire a new generation of readers!

* Van's unmistakable humor and hard-hitting truths will rejuvenate readers to let the past go, learn from their mistakes, and reach higher to achieve their dreams.

* Internationally known motivational speaker and author, Van Crouch travels and speaks across America and the world to professional and collegiate sports organizations, Fortune 500 companies, management and sales conventions, and nationally known ministries.

VAN CROUCH

is widely regarded as one of the best and more versatile speakers in America. As the founder and president of the consulting firm, Van Crouch Communications, Van challenges individuals to achieve excellence in their lives. After ranking as a consistent sales leader with the American Express Company, Van went on to receive many awards for outstanding performance in the insurance industry and has been a qualifying member of the Million Dollar Round Table. Van is the author of several bestselling books including *Stay in the Game*, *Dare to Succeed*, *Take It Back*, *Winning 101*, and *The C.E.O. 's Little Instruction Book*. Van is in demand for his thought-provoking seminars and keynote engagements to Fortune 500 companies, government organizations, professional and collegiate sports teams, church groups, and management and sales conventions worldwide. Van resides with his wife, Donnie, in Wheaton, Illinois.

Daily Insights to Help You Achieve Excellence!

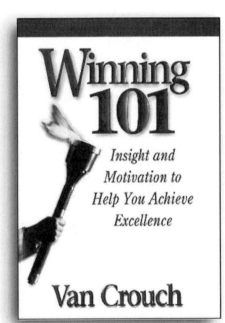

Author Van Crouch encourages readers to overcome obstacles, aim for excellence, and become achievers through these dynamic one-page devotions.

Winning 101 will help you get the daily motivation you need to purse great exploits!

5" x 7" Hard cover
320 pages $14.99 suggested retail
ISBN-13: 978-1-56292-457-7

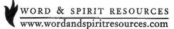